PLEASE RETURN TO
MRS. KRIKORIAN

·PICTURES OF THE PAST·

The Egyptians

Denise Allard

Gareth Stevens Publishing
MILWAUKEE

For a free color catalog describing Gareth Stevens Publishing's list of high-quality books and multimedia programs, call 1-800-542-2595 (USA) or 1-800-461-9120 (Canada). Gareth Stevens Publishing's Fax: (414) 225-0377. See our catalog, too, on the World Wide Web: http://gsinc.com

Library of Congress Cataloging-in-Publication Data

Allard, Denise, 1952-
    The Egyptians / Denise Allard.
        p. cm. — (Pictures of the past)
    Includes index.
    Summary: Describes various aspects of life in ancient Egypt,
including homes and families, farming, towns, building,
recreation, and religion.
    ISBN 0-8368-1714-1 (lib. bdg.)
    1. Egypt—Civilization—To 332 B.C.—Juvenile literature.
[I. Egypt—Civilization—To 332 B.C.] I. Title. II. Series:
Pictures of the past (Milwaukee, Wis.)
DT61.A4989   1997
932—dc21   96-46378

This edition first published in 1997 by
Gareth Stevens Publishing
1555 North RiverCenter Drive, Suite 201
Milwaukee, Wisconsin 53212 USA

Original © 1995 Zoë Books Limited, 15 Worthy Lane, Winchester, Hampshire,
SO23 7AB, England. Additional end matter © 1997 by Gareth Stevens, Inc.

Illustrations: Richard Hook and Clive Spong

The publishers wish to acknowledge, with thanks, the Hutchison Library/
Jeremy A. Horner for the use of the photograph on page 6.

Printed in the United States of America

1 2 3 4 5 6 7 8 9 01 00 99 98 97

Contents

Egypt

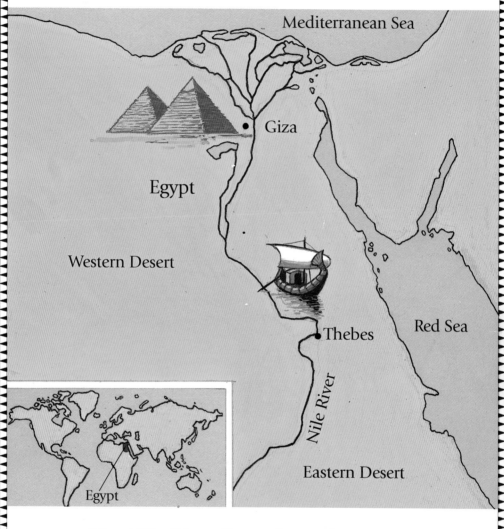

The Nile River flows through Egypt.
Can you find the river on the map?

Egypt

Egypt is a dry and hot country.
Very little rain falls there.
Most of the water in Egypt
comes from the Nile River.
People in Egypt use water
from the Nile for washing
and cooking.

The Nile River provides
water to grow crops, as well.
Without water from the Nile,
it would not be possible for
people to live in Egypt.

Long ago

The pyramids and the sphinx were
built in Egypt long ago.

Long ago

Researchers have learned about the ancient Egyptians from the objects the Egyptians left behind.

Many tourists visit Egypt on their vacations. They see the buildings that people of Egypt built a long time ago.

At home

It was cooler on the roof of a house
than inside.

At home

Family life was important in
ancient Egypt. The women
looked after the children
and did all the housework.
In poor homes, everyone did
some type of work.

Houses were built from mud
bricks and had flat roofs.
Rooms had small windows
to keep out the sun.

Children and work

What types of jobs do you think
people had long ago?

Children and work

Most Egyptian children did
not go to school. They often
did the same work as their
parents. They learned how to
make items or how to farm.

Some boys and girls did go
to school until age thirteen.
They learned how to read
and write.

Writing

Try writing to a friend using only pictures instead of words.

Writing

The ancient Egyptians were one of the first peoples to write. They wrote on paper with pen and ink. The men who did the writing were called scribes.

The scribes did not use the alphabet. They drew small pictures instead. People spent years learning to write.

Farming

These workers are harvesting a crop.
Each one has a special job.

Farming

In ancient Egypt, most people worked the land. They grew vegetables and fruits.

Farmers used a machine called a *shaduf* to lift water from the Nile River for the crops. *Shadufs* are still used today.

The Nile River

Fishing the Nile was an important
job for ancient Egyptians.

The Nile River

People sailed from place
to place on the Nile River.
They caught fish to eat.
They also made items, such
as paper, from the reeds
that grew on the riverbank.

All types of boats sailed
the Nile. Some were very
large. Many of them
had colorful sails.

In towns

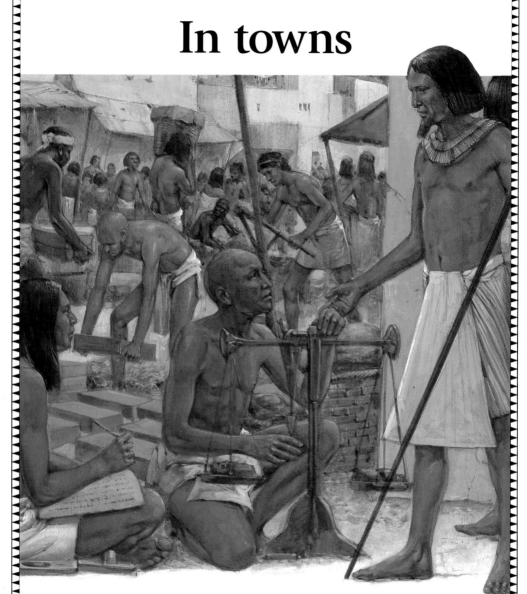

In ancient Egypt, people traded for
the items they needed.

In towns

Each town in ancient Egypt had a marketplace with shops. Offices and royal palaces were also in town.

Money was not in use during early times in Egypt.

Making items

Ancient Egyptians had many uses for clay pots.

Making items

Some people earned their living by making tools, pots, shoes, and cloth.

Ancient Egyptians made clay pots using a wheel. The wheel turned around as the worker shaped the pot.

Parties

Egyptians enjoyed parties. They wore
their finest jewelry to attend.

Parties

Music, dancing, and food were the highlights of parties in ancient Egypt. People ate meat, vegetables, fruits, and cheeses. They drank wine and beer.

Most clothes in ancient Egypt were very plain. But rich Egyptians wore jewelry and makeup.

Games and sports

Egyptians hunted birds and other
animals that lived near the Nile.

Games and sports

Ancient Egyptians enjoyed board games, and they loved to dance.

Children played with dolls and model boats. They also played games such as leapfrog and catch.

A new life

In Egypt, valuables were buried with
the dead for use in the next life.

A new life

Ancient Egyptians thought
people went to another life
after death. They wrapped
the dead in bandages and
buried them with everything
they needed for a new life.

Rich Egyptians were buried
in secret rooms underground.
These rooms are sometimes
discovered in modern times
with the treasure still there.

Pyramids

The pyramids are some of the
magnificent wonders of our world.

Pyramids

Ancient Egyptians were ruled by a king or queen called a pharaoh. People thought the pharaoh was a god or goddess. When they died, some of these pharaohs were buried inside huge pyramids.

Ancient Egyptians did not have machines to build pyramids. They moved the huge stones by hand.

Gods and goddesses

The Ancient Egyptians believed in many gods and goddesses.

Amon: the king of the gods and goddesses. He looked after the pharaoh.

Anubis: the god of dead people.

Bast: the goddess of music and dance.

Geb: the god of the earth.

Hathor: the goddess of the sky. She looked after women.

Horus: the god of Lower Egypt. He looked after the pharaoh.

Isis: the queen of the gods and goddesses.

Min: the god of farming.

Osiris: the husband of Isis and the father of Horus.

Re: the god of the Sun.

Books

Egyptian Tombs. Jeanne Bendick (Watts)

Everyday Life in Ancient Egypt. Anne Pearson (Watts)

The Great Pyramids and the Sphinx. Tony Smith (International Book Center)

Growing Up in Ancient Egypt. Rosalie David (Troll Communications)

Videos

Egypt: Gift of the Nile. (Agency for Instructional Technology)

Mummies Made in Egypt. (Great Plains National Instructional Television Library)

The Mystery of the Pyramids. (Barr Films)

Web Sites

http://www.seas.upenn.edu/%7Eahm/history.htm

http://www.ed.gov/pubs/parents/History/Home.html

Index